He huinga nō ngā maunga puta noa i te ao.
We are many people from throughout the world

Kotahi te iwi.
– one people –

Kotahi te takahi i tēnei whenua ahurei.
walking together in this unique country.

KERRY FOX

Millennium dawn landing at Midway Beach West, features a traditional Maori welcome to a host of waka and sailing canoes from around the Pacific, followed by the tall ship 'The Spirit of New Zealand'. GISBORNE

A RANDOM HOUSE BOOK

Published by
Random House New Zealand
18 Poland Road, Glenfield, Auckland, New Zealand

First published 2000

ISBN 186941 422 5

Conceived and produced for the publishers by
J.M. McGregor Ltd, PO Box 3015, Auckland, New Zealand.

Originator, Producer and Editor-in-Chief: Malcolm McGregor
Project Coordinator: Brian Curtis
Print Consultant: Mark Garner
Editor: Jeannie McGregor
Introduction: Anna Carter
Design and Artwork: Garner Graphics, Sydney
Cover Design: Dexter Fry
Film Processing: Imageworks, Auckland
Colour Separation and Film: Independent Litho, Sydney
Printed in China by Everbest Printing Co Ltd

Participating photographers used FUJI film

We are grateful for the assistance of

A
Day
IN THE
LIFE OF
NEW ZEALAND

THE FIRST DAY OF THE NEW MILLENNIUM

RANDOM HOUSE
NEW ZEALAND

*A*s New Zealand steps over the threshold into a new century and millennium, it is evident that we are a very different society from that of even a decade ago. Technology and affordable travel have given New Zealanders instant access to the wider world and our physical isolation is no longer a significant factor in our culture. Yet while we have become more cosmopolitan, more sophisticated and more worldly, the distinctive national identity of the Kiwi prevails. We are a multi-cultural society characterised as unpretentious, adept and adventurous, with the ability to turn our hands to anything.

It was in the earliest days of European settlement that the character of today's New Zealander was forged. To survive in a new land three main qualities were required, independence, self-reliance and adaptability. Qualities just as urgently needed today as we embark on a new era.

New Zealand's cultural identity draws together a multitude of influences from our indigenous Maori culture, our Pacific Island neighbours and our origins as a British colony, creating a unique and individual character.

We may have developed in a relatively insular environment but, over the past two decades, the Pakeha psyche has grown beyond its former dependence on England. A Maori renaissance has guaranteed potent political debate and a predominantly Polynesian and Asian immigrant society, together with major influxes from Mediterranean regions, has seen that rather than becoming a pale imitation of a Euro-American civilisation, New Zealand continues to be different and diverse. We are now learning to live with a new, yet still unique identity. We have our own distinctive art, literature, dialects and living style and, as we emerge into a new millennium, there is evidence of a renewed energy and confidence in our individuality.

For a tiny country, New Zealand's natural environment is also wonderfully diverse – alpine peaks, lakes, glaciers and rain forests, grassy plains, golden beaches and that peculiarity of New Zealand animal life – the almost complete lack of native mammals. Since the separation of the islands from other land masses over millions of years, the country has been so isolated that the lack of serious predators has led to the evolution of many unusual creatures, in particular flightless birds including the nocturnal Kiwi, our national emblem. Isolation has also led to the evolution of new and unique species of plant life and the emergence of ancient species that have died out elsewhere. Of the approximately 2000 native plant species here, nearly three-quarters are found nowhere else in the world.

The land too is unique. New Zealand's spectacularly beautiful landscape incorporates vast mountain chains, steaming volcanoes, sweeping coasts, deeply indented fiords and fertile, well-farmed green pastures. Equivalent in size to Great Britain, California or Japan, we are a population of only 3.8 million, making ours one of the world's least crowded countries – a haven for those seeking peace, rejuvenation and relaxation. It is also a playground for those seeking thrills and adventure.

But it is through the Kiwi culture that you really discover the true spirit of our country. New Zealand gave the world firsts in almost every field – sport, science, education, women's franchise and, yes, bungy jumping, jet boating, kiwifruit, world class wines, millions of sheep… and the first light of the new millennium. Whilst our national sport is the physical, rough-and-tumble game of rugby, Kiwis also love a good espresso and our arts festivals are international draw cards. Our writers, designers, artists, musicians and movies enjoy international acclaim and as we usher in a new epoch, the image of New Zealanders as inventive, free-spirited and fun loving is as true today as it was a century ago. These qualities and the diversity of our nation are reflected in this important volume, employing the skills of 80 of our best and most imaginative photographers, providing a record for generations to come.

The rain parts for a few seconds as the sun breaks the horizon. AUCKLAND

KERRY FOX

■ GISBORNE

It seems the whole nation began the 21st century with a party despite the weather. Fireworks figured prominently in most of the celebrations.

■ WELLINGTON

Caroline Bay Carnival. TIMARU

KERRY FOX

■ Auld Lang Syne – Mayor John Clarke, wife
Barbara, Town Cryer John Dwight and wife Mary
at the Town Clock Party. GISBORNE

BRUCE JENKINS

■ Entering into the spirit. ESKDALE

■ Karangahape Road nightclubbers. AUCKLAND

■ Fancy dress party at Bannockburn. CENTRAL OTAGO

Partying on at Millbrook Resort. QUEENSTOWN

■ Peter Snell assists
with New Year
celebrations. He was
in Feilding for the
World Masters
Orienteering, the first
athletic event of the
new millennium, in
which competitors
from 20 countries
participated. FEILDING

LIZ BROOK

■ WAIMANGAROA

TONY FERGUSON

Piping in the new year in front of the Town Hall. The southern provinces of New Zealand are amongst the few places in the world where New Year, or Hogmanay, is celebrated in traditional Scottish fashion. The Dunedin Town Hall is built of Oamaru stone and contains the country's finest turret chiming clock. DUNEDIN

JANE DAWBER

■ Julian Smith, Managing Director of the 'Otago Daily Times'. DUNEDIN

■ Midnight: Julian Smith and Kenny Whyte appear to merge into one as they fire Julian's antique cannon on a hilltop overlooking Warrington and Waitati Inlet. WAITATI

KEVIN WEIR

MATHESON BEAUMONT

■ **Visitors from Las Vegas at Millbrook Resort.** QUEENSTOWN

DENIS PAGÉ

As if it isn't difficult enough at any time! Midnight golf at the Russley Golf Course for pro Craig Mitchell. CHRISTCHURCH

American legend, Stan Fox, was first away in the first motorsport event of the millennium, a 20 lap allcomers event at Pukekohe Park Raceway won by local driver 'Racing Ray Williams'. PUKEKOHE

■ First bungy jump! Colin Basterfield from Oxfordshire, UK, paid $4,500 to make the first bungy jump of the new millennium. (Sponsored by Esoft). QUEENSTOWN

SHEENA HAYWOOD

Grand Chateau Annual Ball. TONGARIRO NATIONAL PARK

■ Singer John Rowles leads the celebration in the Square. FEILDING

MICHAEL MATTHEW

■ David and Eva from
FIREworks, professional
fire performers in the
fire pit, a huge natural
sinkhole, at The
Gathering. TAKAKA

■ TVNZ news room.
AUCKLAND

STEPHEN ROBINSON

Meditation at midnight. CANTERBURY

■ Samoan mass at the Cathedral of
the Blessed Sacrament. CHRISTCHURCH

Dancing the night away. TIRAUMEA

■ Fancy dress party at Bannockburn.
CENTRAL OTAGO

■ The first sheep to be shorn and fleece to be
spun in the new millennium. Modern technology
not required. MASTERTON

■ Participant in 'Dances of Life',
Convergence 2000. NORTH LOBURN

■ "It works!"
Whaiti Albert. KERIKERI

AVIS MOUNTAIN

Dinner party at the home of Tom and Suzy Van der Kwast. Among the group are Dutch and German migrants most of whom came to New Zealand in the fifties. WELLINGTON

Saving water? CANTERBURY

JANE DAWBER

■ Bill Lucas (42) finishes the 19 circuits of Logan Park in the first marathon of the new century. Twelve keen Dunedin athletes started as the clock ticked over at 12 midnight and first home was Richard Hendry. Although Bill ran barefoot, his feet suffered no cuts or blisters as he regularly trains barefoot. DUNEDIN

■ Survivors of the 2000 dip! TIMARU

CRAIG PERKINS

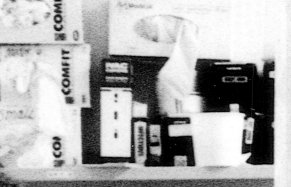

Middlemore Hospital, A & B Ward.
AUCKLAND

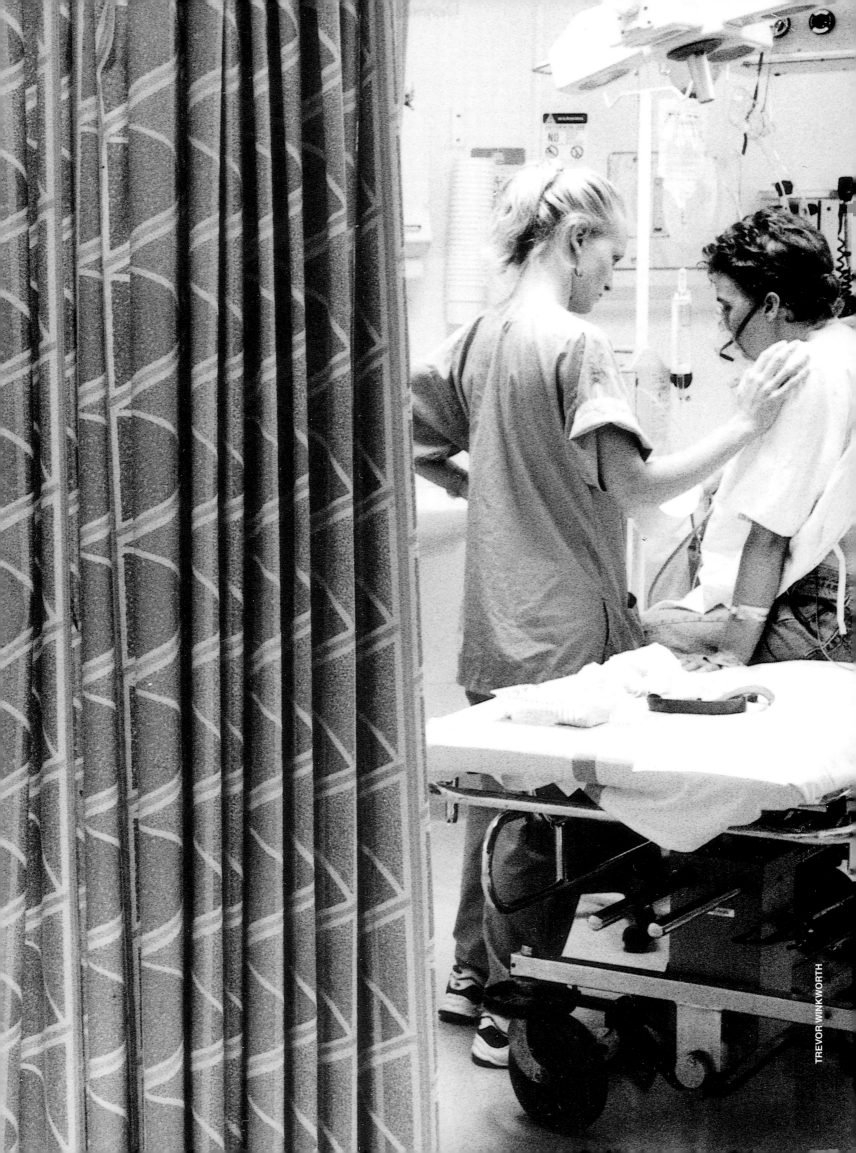

KERRY FOX

■ Dame Kiri Te Kanawa and music director of the New Zealand
Symphony Orchestra, James Judd, at Ruamano 2000, Millennium
Dawn Ceremony. GISBORNE

SIMON WOOLF

■ Sir Michael Hardie-Boys, Governor General of New Zealand, greets former
Prime Minister, Jenny Shipley at dawn ceremony at Te Papa. WELLINGTON

KEVIN WEIR

■ Sandra Auld and Lawrie Forbes tie
the knot at Signal Hill Lookout. DUNEDIN

■ Sky Tower disappears into the mist. AUCKLAND

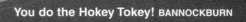

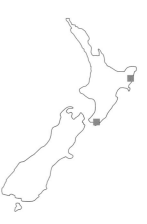

■ Dawn ceremony at Te Papa.
WELLINGTON

KERRY FOX

■ Award-winning dancer, Annalise Morris, and her
troup of 12, perform at the Town Clock Party. GISBORNE

■ Sunrise at the Anzac Memorial on top of the Taipo hills at Tinui. The grandfather of the young man helped erect the original wooden cross in April 1916. WAIRARAPA

RON REDFERN

■ Piper Bruce Stuart on Smith's Hill. TIRAUMEA

Waiting for sunrise. QUEENSTOWN

■ Maika Te Amo welcomes the
dawn of a new millennium. MAKETU

■ Hot springs. MARUIA

■ The Gathering is a huge outdoor rave or dance party in the hills of Takaka. No alcohol is allowed into the remote location, 1000 metres above sea level, which adds to the peaceful, happy feelings and lack of crime and violence. It is an annual event, with about 200 performers and 13,000 people attending, including a crew of 1100. This year the event was a washout – torrential rain made the site a sea of mud and 12 people were treated for hypothermia.
CANAAN DOWNS. TAKAKA

NICK SERVIAN

5:45am: A group of Americans on Cecil Peak,
3200 metres, waiting to greet the sun. QUEENSTOWN

ANTHONY MCKEE

■ The first dawn of the new millennium – and the
first inhabited land mass in the world to feel the sun's
rays, 45 minutes ahead of the rest of New Zealand.
CHATHAM ISLANDS

ANTHONY McKEE

■ At Rangaika, Andre Day (17) blows a traditional conch to greet the rising sun. A similar picture was seen by billions of people as it was beamed around the world. CHATHAM ISLANDS

The Mayor of Wellington, Mark Blumsky, with some of the 1000 children from 88 countries welcoming the dawn on Mt Victoria in an internationally televised ceremony. WELLINGTON

ANTHONY MCKEE

■ Christoper Solomon (10), Louis Tipene (8) and George Solomon (11), all from Auckland, wait against the light of dawn to perform with their grandfather in a Moriori ceremony at Rangaika. CHATHAM ISLANDS

■ Fun at the first sunrise in Hawkes Bay.
NAPIER

BRUCE JENKINS

Dawn at Whirinaki Beach, HAWKES BAY

■ Not everyone needs
a hotel bed. QUEENSTOWN

■ Main tent at Convergence 2000, a movement attempting to resolve life issues. It began 15 years ago and has been leading up to the year 2000. Everyone at Convergence is totally alcohol and drug free. JOURNEYS END, NORTH LOBURN

MARK HAMILTON

■ Warming up on Smiths Hill. TIRAUMEA

■ Gary and Nancy Caskey from Wisconsin celebrate sunrise at Cecil Peak Station. QUEENSTOWN

■ Participants in the world's first polo game of the new millennium: Gillian Thom (Dubai, UAE), Lachlan Mackinnon (Australia), Mark Harris (NZ), Gerald Kagan (USA), Andy Thom (Dubai UAE), James Neary (England), Mark Donald (NZ) and Jan van de Pol (England). TUAHIWI

BRIAN CURTIS

■ Arriving for the dawn ceremony. AUCKLAND HARBOUR

Maori waka landing in dawn ceremony at Okahu Bay. AUCKLAND

■ Basic accommodation. CANTERBURY

The cold couldn't cool the spirits! Some of
New Zealand's contingent at Scott Base.
ANTARCTICA

SHEENA HAYWOOD

Maree Cross and her daughter, Holly Tatom-Cross, wait for the arrival of Louis, born at 11.27am on 1.1.2000. QUEENSTOWN

KIM REED

■ Brownie Hodge, in town for the rodeo. KAITAIA

■ Ron McTaggert, a miner for 42 years. RUNANGA

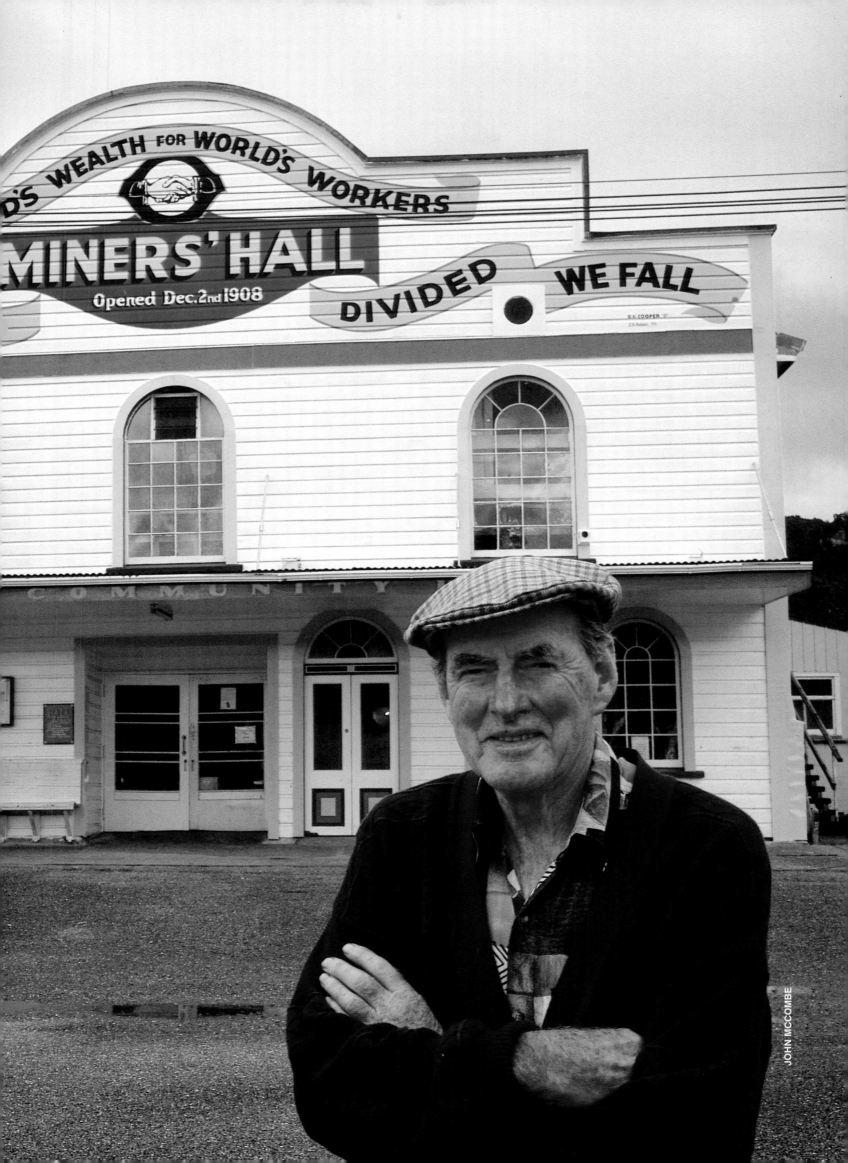

D'S WEALTH FOR WORLD'S WORKERS

MINERS' HALL

Opened Dec. 2nd 1908

DIVIDED WE FALL

■ **Disembarking at 9:00am after a New Year's Eve cruise on Milford Sound.** MILFORD

SONYA CROOK

■ On the Shotover River.
QUEENSTOWN

■ Paddlesteamer 'Waimarie' on its maiden journey after being recommissioned at midnight. WHANGANUI RIVER

Joanne Borrie and her sons Lister and Oliver watch the
New Year's Day regatta from the headland. MANGONUI

■ Beats bikes! Coannon
Roberts (front), Piwa Tuaupiki
and Haami Tuaupiki (right) at
Te Maka. KAWHIA HARBOUR

■ Rebecca-Lynn – the
island's own Y2K bug.
STEWART ISLAND

LAURA CAVANAGH

The mobile village of Atchintan consists of 45 families of gypsies who are living their dream, travelling the country in their unique homes, surviving on their talents.
ATCHINTAN AT COROMANDEL

■ Heading for the Clutha River on a fishing/camping expedition. ALBERTOWN

GILBERT VAN REENEN

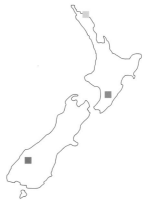

■ Road stop for Robert and Ann Campbell. EKETAHUNA

■ Children of the New Dawn Cultural Group in the Waitangi Treaty Grounds. BAY OF ISLANDS

91

"We'll win it again this year girls!" Sheree and Dylan Ditchfield with son Blake. SOUTHLAND

Leon Searles and his created world of flotsam and jetsam. He and his wife, Lorraine, collect material daily from nearby Baylys Beach.
KAIPARA HARBOUR

Margaret Henderikson, permanent resident of Onaero Motor Camp.
NEAR NEW PLYMOUTH

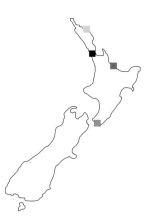

KEVIN STENT

■ Tevita Sovea, 10 years old and his pure albino brother Abraham, aged one, both with the same parents. WELLINGTON

■ TAURANGA

■ At the millennium celebrations. AUCKLAND

CHRIS PARKER

NEIL FARRIN

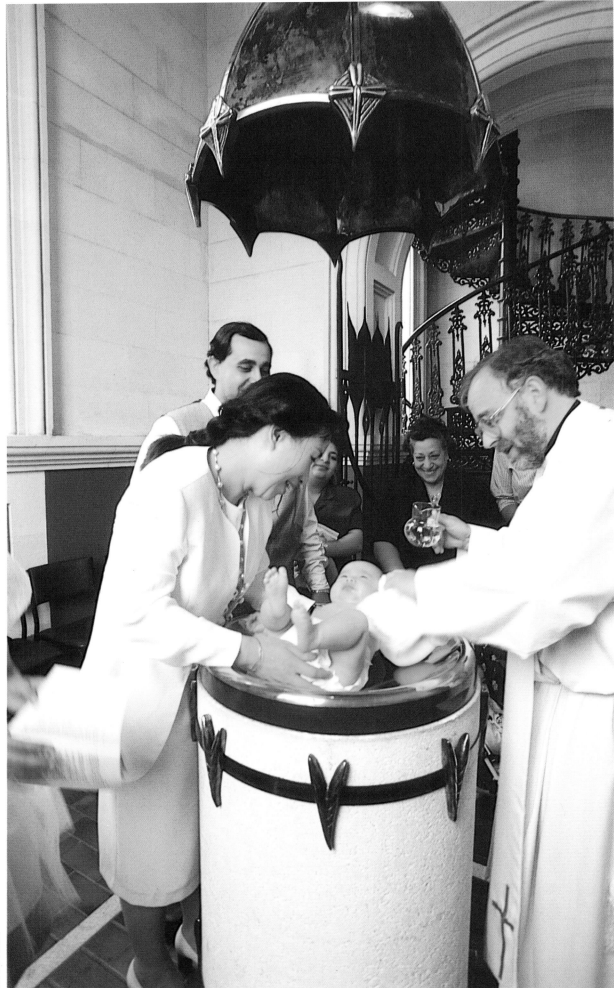

■ Father Rick baptises Vivien Wassim Emile, daughter of Dr W. Emile (Egyptian) and mother Ke Feng (Chinese) at the Cathedral of the Blessed Sacrament. CHRISTCHURCH

■ Ingestre Street Church of Christ baptism service.
WHANGANUI RIVER

■ **Keeping cool!**
Savannah Sandlant,
three years old.
OMANU, MT MAUNGANUI

■ On duty – saving lives.
GISBORNE

■ NZ cricket captain
2020? MURIWAI

107

'Olveston', a Jacobean style mansion, was built in 1904 and bequeathed by the Theomin family to the City of Dunedin, complete with original furnishings and art treasures. It is open to the public and provides a delightful glimpse of life in the early 1900s. DUNEDIN

■ Home of champions
– Cambridge Stud.
RIGHT: a permanent
memorial to an icon of
New Zealand racing.
BELOW: Zabeel, son of Sir
Tristram, with Gary
Mudgway. This famous
sire is proving almost as
successful as his father.
CAMBRIDGE

■ Stuart Landsborough with his extraordinary
'Maze and Puzzling World'. WANAKA

Tania Crook, primate keeper at Auckland Zoo, hand feeds the Tamarins. These monkeys are not enclosed at all and are hand fed every day in the same area of the zoo. They are free to roam anywhere but choose to stay in the one area. AUCKLAND

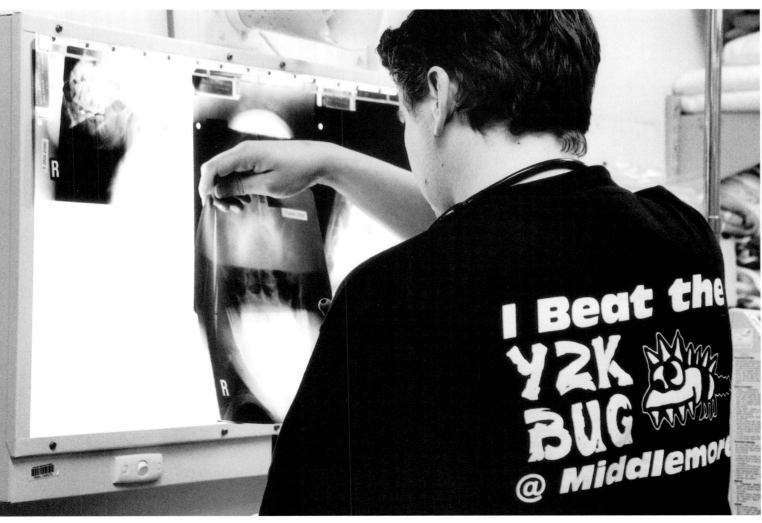

■ Dorita Mangu, Doreen Shelton and Gerald McLeod on duty. BLUFF

■ After midnight at Middlemore Hospital, everyone donned their 'I beat the Y2K Bug' T-shirts. AUCKLAND

■ Ivy Spiers (104) has lived in three centuries. She wrote her autobiography at the age of 99 and took up porcelain painting at 87. She and her husband farmed in the Horowhenua district where Mrs Spiers was a show cattle judge. FEILDING

■ Two-year-old Laura with her mother Carolyn Ambags, who gives her time unconditionally to care for her daughter. Recent tests indicate that Laura is responding positively to treatment at Star Ship Children's Hospital. AUCKLAND

Tania Kay, bellringer
at St Paul's Church.
INVERCARGILL

LAKE TAUPO

Refreshment break at the Moth Restaurant. MANDEVILLE

ARTHUR BREMFORD

■ RIGHT: A new design for Master Carver Tuti Tukaokao
BELOW: Tuti with good friend Topsy.
BAY OF PLENTY

■ Barry Brickell, professional potter, works on a sculpture at the terminus of his Driving Creek Bush Railway. COROMANDEL

Graham Taylor, gill netter. KAWHIA

■ There'll always be an England! Mark and Wendy Dukes with Max and Bob, father and son champion breed bulldogs. OPUNAKE

■ Walaalaha Somali Soccer Team competing in a tournament at Waikato University. HAMILTON

MILLS WORLD OF FITNESS

LITEACE

UE3205

Where did you come from? WELLINGTON

PETER BUSH

A bloke and his shed! Vincenzo Criscillo (93), was born on the island of Stromboli, Italy, and came to New Zealand as a young man. WELLINGTON

COROMANDEL

Jenny Cameron, Emma Jolley, Rebecca Ganley and Carla Bridge – all from Palmerston North. LAKE TAUPO

■ Local teacher Dave Waugh with the 'Kurow Hay People' which are a tradition in the area.
KUROW

SHEENA HAYWOOD

■ Three generations of one family – Ken Brosnan, his son Alister and grandson James.
FERNSIDE

CYNTHIA VAN DE LOO

Feeding time at
Orana Park Wildlife
Trust. CANTERBURY

Beaconsfield Valley. MANAWATŪ

■ At 102, Edith Burch has lived in three centuries. She is interviewed by 'Evening Standard' reporter, Nicola Boges, at a champagne breakfast in the Square.
PALMERSTON NORTH

■ 'Tarts on Tour'. Viv Speedy (Auckland), Sarah Chevin (Zimbabwe) and Leslie Gaston (Mahoenui), hamming it up.
QUEENSTOWN

A three-year-old millennium angel! QUEENSTOWN

'Three Men and a Baby'! Best friends Jesse Henry, Bernie White and Brian Roderique with their baby 'Keg' doing the rounds of the pubs.
BLUFF

KAREN JOHNSON

KING OF THE ROAD

AUCKLAND

■ Conductor's assistant at Ellerslie races. AUCKLAND

■ Band of the Royal New Zealand Navy in the
Waitangi Treaty Grounds. BAY OF ISLANDS

■ Embellishments.
COROMANDEL

■ Tatai Kerr-Tuaupiki and
friends. KAWHIA HARBOUR

GERAR TOYS

RHYS PALMER

140

■ Lucas Williams would rather watch than play petanque. OHOKA

Panning for millennium gold – David Hardy with assistant Brooke Webster. ARROWTOWN

■ Lucky visitors to the
Tank Hall at Cloudy Bay
vineyards sampling one
of New Zealand's medal-
winning wines. Cloudy
Bay wines are renowned
throughout the world.
BLENHEIM

KEVIN JUDD

■ Grant McMaster and
Peter Standish outside
the Waikaia Hotel and the
old post office. WAIKAIA

ARTHUR BREMFORD

■ Tom Richardson's tractor has a special gadget to pick up hay bales. They are in a race with the rain which is threatening. FEILDING

■ Argyle Station cattle drive. SOUTHLAND

■ Gaye Jellie in a field of Sandersonia. OHAUPO

EDWIN EMERY

■ Rosie Gill and children, Mariel, Malcolm and Eilidh, from Otautau, after a walk up to the Tasman Glacier lookout. MT COOK

■ Flower laden fairy at America's Cup Village, Viaduct Basin. AUCKLAND

■ One man band at quiet America's Cup Village. New Year's Day is a day of rest for yachtsmen taking part in the challenger series semi-finals of the Louis Vuitton Cup, commencing 2nd January 2000, to determine who will sail against Team New Zealand for the America's Cup. AUCKLAND

...ve supplied a number of children with Fujicolor QuickSnap Super 800 single-use cameras on the day. These are some of the results.

Thomas Poole (10)

Abigail Poole (12)

ABOVE AND LEFT:
Jamie Moffatt (11)
Jamie turned 11 on 1.1.2000

Dina Wuest (5)

Rhys Applegarth (9)

Christina Stenning (7)

Courtney Dawson (11)

■ 'Miss Taranaki Beach
Resort' contestants at
Oakura Beach Carnival.
TARANAKI

■ 'Junior Mr Muscle' at
Oakura Beach. TARANAKI

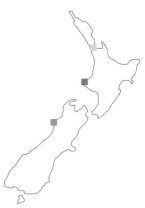

■ Mickey and Bev Hawes, owners of Kynersley Tavern, with a model of an America's Cup yacht which took 100 hours to build from a fence post. MOKIHINUI

■ A successful fisherman! Cousins Tyrone Driver and Shenice Sue at Birkenhead Wharf. AUCKLAND

KIRBY WRIGHT

■ Taz with Carole Harvey at the Kiwi House, Rainbow Springs, Rotorua. Taz is part of the kiwi survival programme Operation Nest. ROTORUA

■ Built to last. WAITANGI

■ 'Golden Butterfly' is led around the birdcage. HASTINGS

Auckland Cup Day: Leigh McGregor and friends outside the Polo Bar, Members Stand, Auckland Racing Club. After heavy rain and a horse falling in Race 3, the race meeting was postponed due to the condition of the track which resulted in the postponement of the Auckland Cup for the first time in its history. ELLERSLIE

Grim determination. New
Year Sports Day. TUATAPERE

Judy Webby, President of Kapiti Rotary Club plants a tree to mark the burying of a millennium time capsule beside State Highway 1. It is planned that the capsule will be re-opened in 2100. NORTH OF PARAPARAUMU

The chips fly in a millennium wood chopping competition. OPONONI, HOKIANGA

■ A well known voice in the area – Maria Eynon,
D.J. Bay Radio 100.2. AKAROA

■ Ellen Hopkins, aged 96. Mrs. Hopkins has photographed Akaroa for the last 57 years. AKAROA

■ The ultimate informal herb garden! Lynne Alexander has every variety imaginable. AKAROA

■ A magic moment – on board inter-island ferry 'Arahura'. COOK STRAIT

■ Fish are biting!
TAURANGA

CHRIS PARKER

■ M.P. and Mayor of
Carterton, Georgina
Beyer, is interviewed by
TV One. CARTERTON

Original artwork on
One Tree Hill. AUCKLAND

NEIL FARRIN

164

CRAIG FERGUS

■ 'Miss Caroline Bay'.
TIMARU

■ Celebration of men
and women coming
together, trying to bridge
the gap, at Convergence
2000. NORTH LOBURN

CYNTHIA VAN DER LOO

165

■ Michael Brajkovich celebrates his birthday with his family. KUMEU

■ BELOW: FNDC Mayor Yvonne Sharp conducts a citizenship ceremony at Whare Runanga. Each new citizen later planted a tree.
LEFT: The first new citizen of the millennium, six-year-old Kimberley-Jade Larkan from South Africa, with Mayor Yvonne Sharp. WAITANGI

■ Noela Weir finds herself at the wrong end of their Model A car with husband Allan in the driver's seat.
WEST COAST, SOUTH ISLAND

■ Joe Fox on his
moped – going home.
GISBORNE

■ Tony Wass (left) and
Gary Dover, with their
1959 Ford Edsel hard
top classics, in the
National Street Rod
Association 2000 Coast
to Coast Sunrise to
Sunset competition.
SOUTH TARANAKI

George Herbert, captain of the 'Earnslaw' which plies Lake Wakatipu. QUEENSTOWN

GRAEME SEDAL

■ After a busy first day of the new millennium – from Mt Hikurangi at dawn, Gisborne, and on to the Auckland race meeting – Helen Clark, Prime Minister of New Zealand, relaxes before an evening meal with her husband and friends at the America's Cup Village. AUCKLAND

■ Lex Anson, Chief Concierge Hyatt Regency Hotel. AUCKLAND

BRIAN CURTIS

■ Owner of Larnach Castle, Margaret Barker, having just planted a tree to mark the new millennium. Larnach Castle was built in the 1870s and has about 40 rooms spread over 3,716 square metres. The castle is open to the public for inspection.
DUNEDIN

■ Father Ilian in St Michaels Orthodox Church, which is used by both Greek and Russian Orthodox communities as well as the Lebanese community. SOUTH DUNEDIN

GEOFF O'BRIEN

■ Coptic Orthodox families are delighted to participate in the first Coptic liturgy of the millennium with their esteemed guests from Egypt and Australia. The Coptic Orthodox Church has around 10 million members worldwide. L to r: Bishop Asheia (Egypt), Bishop Suriel (Australia) and Father Sourial Youssef (Christchurch).
CHRISTCHURCH

175

176

■ Graeme and Jean Robertson live in what is known locally as 'the can house'. Graeme is an avid collector of beer cans from around the world and in 1984 he started to attach them to his ceilings. He now has a grand total of 5772 cans attached – a sight to behold. INVERCARGILL

■ Glenn Anderson, designer of a four-wheel-drive dirt board – a first in the world. KAIAPOI

■ Becky Fowler on her last day as the 'Earnslaw' pianist. Becky, aged 72, has been playing the piano on the 'Earnslaw' for 17 years. Sarah Chevin from Zimbabwe is obviously enjoying it! QUEENSTOWN

CYNTHIA VAN DE LOO

RICHARD POOLE

■ Retired fisheries ship's captain, 75-year-old Mr Loo-Chi Hu, Go player, Tai Chi instructor and 1955 America's Cup challenger – in a 78ft Chinese Junk! CHRISTCHURCH

■ Nita Mills turned 101 on 1.1.2000. Her family mistakenly thought they were celebrating her 100th birthday until her son took a closer look at her birth certificate! INVERCARGILL

■ Isabella Kelly, 93 years old, cared for by her grandson, Paul Winder, a nurse at Southland Hospital. INVERCARGILL

■ City skyline – everchanging. AUCKLAND

■ 'On a fine day you can see forever'. One Tree Hill. AUCKLAND

Maurice Williams reminiscing with a young friend. Maurice is well known throughout the country for his work in TV ads. LAKE HAYES

GABRIELS GULL
"WAGON TRAIN"
CAVALCADE '94

■ Patrons of the Waimate Pub stayed their elbows to have their presence recorded on the day. MANAIA

■ German tourist group in front of Hundertwasser public toilets, which have been decorated by a famous Austrian painter and architect. KAWAKAWA

186

SHEENA HAYWOOD

Golfer Greg Turner reading with his daughter, Charlie (2) at their holiday home at Arthur's Point.
QUEENSTOWN

■ Late night fishing.
MANGONUI

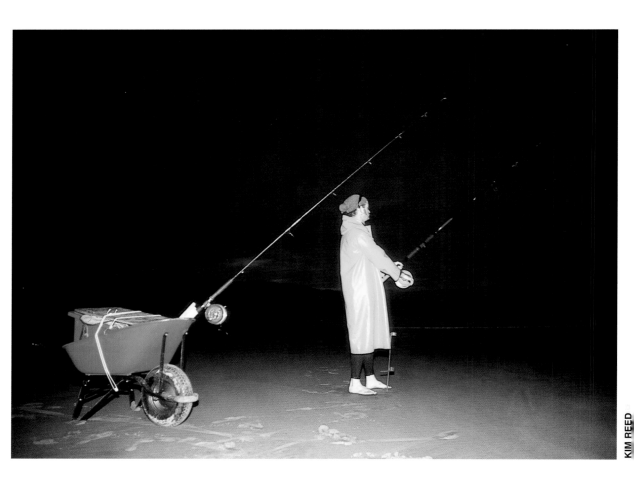

■ Luke Geldermans
kayaks over the 10 metre
Maruia falls for the first
time. "Phew, I'm never
doing that again!" MARUIA

KEVIN WEIR

■ For those who missed out at midnight! Paula Stichman at Casino reception. DUNEDIN

■ Paul Holmes at work on TV One Millennium Special. AUCKLAND

GARY BAILDON

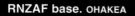
RNZAF base. OHAKEA

OFFICIAL PHOTOGRAPHER
A day in the life of New Zealand
1st January 2000

After shooting all day from midnight: "Feeling like I'd been put through the wringer and hung out to dry." AUCKLAND

GARRY BAILDON

TONY BRIDGE

PAUL DONOVAN

ADRIAN BARRETT

SONYA CROOK

CHRIS DUGGAN

TONY FERGUSON

LIZ BROOK

BRIAN CURTIS

BARRY DURRANT

MATHESON BEAUMONT

PETER BUSH

KERRY FOX

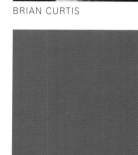

LAURA CAVANAGH

JANE DAWBER

MARK DWYER

JOHN COWPLAND

EDWIN EMERY

GARY BAILDON

Is an account manager with Hanimex NZ Commercial Markets Group. He has been shooting for nearly two decades and has been involved professionally in several disciplines including portraiture, corporate communications and his great passion, motor sport. He adds regularly in his spare time to his diverse collection of stock images.

ADRIAN BARRETT

His creative, photographic and design skills have earned him wide recognition from both the market place and his peers in the NZIPP. His personal commitment to nothing but the best is proven in the list of his achievements over the last 10 years.

MATHESON BEAUMONT

By profession an optometrist in Dunedin, Matheson describes himself as a photographer by avocation. Active in photography since his schooldays, he has an international reputation as a print maker and producer of a/v sequences. His work has been widely exhibited and is held in collections in the UK, Brazil, Singapore, the US and Japan. He has been awarded the Royal Photographic Society Fenton Medal for services to photography, is a Fellow of both the Royal Photographic Society of Great Britain and the Photographic Society of America, and is Chairman of the NZ Centre for Photography. He was a participant in our previous *A Day in the Life of New Zealand* (DITLONZ).

ARTHUR BREMFORD

A photographer, pilot, fisherman, underwater enthusiast, Arthur has operated a studio in Gore for many years. His recent activities have taken him extensively through the Pacific Islands. Also a participant in the original *DITLONZ*.

TONY BRIDGE

Christchurch based, Tony has been in love with photography as long as he can remember and fascinated by the human condition for at least as long. "I think I have the best job in photography – photographing people and teaching others how to make pictures with a camera. What could be more wonderful?"

LIZ BROOK

An icon of the NZ photographic industry, Liz has worked as women's editor and illustrations editor of several major newspapers, as a publicist and is at present communications manager for Hort Research. Liz has won many photography awards, and been published in several books including our original *DITLONZ*.

PETER BUSH

Graduating from a schoolboy box brownie, Peter joined *The New Zealand Herald* and the old *Weekly News*, learning his photojournalistic trade from the ground up. He worked for several government departments and did a stint in Malaya with the army before working for *Truth* and *The Sunday News*. He is particularly noted for his sports photography, rugby being his passion including the recent World Cup. He was one of the participants in the original *DITLONZ*.

LAURA CAVANAGH

At 19 years of age, Laura is our youngest contributor. Resident on Stewart Island, she is sold on its unique lifestyle and unspoiled beauty. She is currently studying journalism.

JOHN COWPLAND

Has been a press photographer for the last six years after training as a RNZAF photographer. During this time he has won two Qantas awards, including 1997 Photographer of the Year. As part of this award, John attended the Missouri Photo Workshop, which he descibes as the most worthwhile experience of his career.

JOHN CRAWFORD

Runs a small successful studio in New Plymouth, concentrating mainly on corporate photography nationally and internationally, plus occasional weddings and portraits. He is a fellow of the NZIPP and has received many prestigious awards from the institute. John was also a participant in the original *DITLONZ*.

SONYA CROOK

A Fellow of the NZIPP, Sonya has concentrated of late on illustrative/editorial essays of the people and landscapes of southern New Zealand.

BRIAN CURTIS

With over 40 years in the industry, Brian is one of the better known New Zealand photographers. He worked for *The Sunday Times* and a number of magazines and was an official photographer for the 1974 and 1990 Commonwealth Games. Since 1992, he has been editor, photographer and publisher of *The Photographer's Mail*. One of the team for our original *DITLONZ*, he has been a tower of strength for this latest production.

JANE DAWBER

Has worked for the last 10 years as senior photographer for *The Otago Daily Times* and also operates a commercial photographic business. She has travelled extensively with recent works appearing in *Shot in Africa* and *New Zealand The Millennium*.

PAT DOLAN

Has been a commercial and industrial photographer for almost 50 years. He is particularly well known for his air to air photography and although now virtually retired, Pat still keeps his hand in at the Christchurch studio of Mannering & Associates.

PAUL DONOVAN

Says: "Stills photography is a passion of mine, even though I work as a documentary cameraman. Over the years I have had photos published in various books and magazines but a special highlight was having 12 images included in the first *DITLONZ*. It is special being part of that venture again."

CHRIS DUGGAN

See Southland Photographic Society.

BARRY DURRANT

Began as a cadet on *The Dominion* in 1958, moved to *The New Zealand Herald* and *Weekly News*. He returned to *The Dominion* in 1972, becoming chief photographer. He covered the major events of the era, disasters, royal and sports tours, etc., before, in 1986, setting up his own photography business in Wellington. Barry was also one of our photographers on the original *DITLONZ*.

MARK DWYER

Travelled the world for nine years before settling on photography. He has picked up several national awards and works full time for Taranaki Newspapers.

EDWIN EMERY

Was a participant in our original *DITLONZ* in 1983 when still a student at Wellington Polytechnic. He went on to do a B.Sc. degree in ecology. Although now a school teacher, he continues his interest in photography. Edwin states: "I am a Ngati Maniopoto. I come from Te Kopua near the river Waipa. Our marae is near the Maunga, Kakepuku. The Waikato is part of my roots."

BRYN EVANS

Living in Austria in 1992, watching the plight of Yugoslav refugees fleeing across the border, kindled Bryn's interest in human affairs. Returning to NZ he undertook a diploma in photography and now works as a photo-journalist covering stories in the UK, Bosnia, South Pacific, NZ and latterly East Timor. He supplements this with commercial work throughout NZ.

NEIL FARRIN

Has worked as a photojournalist and commercial photographer for more than 25 years, for much of that time based in Hong Kong. He began his career in England working for the UK Press, *The Times* and *Daily Telegraph* and since then his work has appeared in *Geo*, *Time*, *Newsweek* and many successful books such as *A Day in the Life of Thailand*, *Here be Dragons* and *Planet Vegas*. Having worked on assignments throughout the world, Neil took up residency in New Zealand in 1998, where he initiated and co-ordinated the *New Zealand The Millennium* project. He now runs Shadowcatcher, the Photographers' Gallery in Auckland.

TONY FERGUSON

Works as a freelance photographer and runs a photographic retail store and studio in Westport. He lists himself as a "dyed-in-the-wool West Coaster"

KERRY FOX

Picked up her first camera at the age of 12 and has gone on to win recognition in international and national photography competitions. Her work has been widely published in books, magazines and calendars. She is a resident of Gisborne.

FRANK HABICHT

BRUCE JENKINS

ANTHONY McKEE

RHYS PALMER

GRAEME JENNINGS

GEOFF O'BRIEN

LLOYD PARK

MARK HAMILTON

KAREN JOHNSON

GEOFF MASON

DAWN PATTERSON

LUKE HAWKINS

ALAN KING

HAROLD MASON

CRAIG PERKINS

SHEENA HAYWOOD

NEIL LIVERSEDGE

ANNE MEIN

DENIS PAGÉ

JOHN McCOMBE

VLADIMIR PETROVIC

FRANK HABICHT

Born in Germany, Frank's work has appeared in a large number of international magazines, newspapers, annual and year books. He has worked for television, as in-house photographer for Playboy Club London, and stills photographer with such directors as Polanski and Dassin. He emigrated to New Zealand in 1982 and has several books to his credit.

MICHAEL HALL

Spent most of the 80's travelling and developed a passion for photography culminating in study at Wellington Polytechnic. Since 1990, Michael has built a strong nation-wide client base and a reputation as a specialist in illustrative and people photography. In demand on both sides of the Tasman.

MARK HAMILTON

Photographing for over 10 years, Mark is already published in various books and magazines. He tutors in photography in addition to currently studying towards an arts degree in photography at Waikato Polytechnic.

LUKE HAWKINS

Has been winning photographic competitions since the age of 12, and now at 20 is one of our new breed. Resident of Hokianga, he currently photographs for The Hokianga News and The Northern News. He is very much the outdoorsman.

SHEENA HAYWOOD

Her enthusiasm for photography and skiing is clearly captured in Sheena's winter action imagery and has led to her accreditation at the last four winter Olympics. She delights in photographing people in action, creating lasting impressions with her artistry, such skill enabling her to photograph some of the world's most famous figures. She is a dynamo as all who work with her will attest.

BRUCE JENKINS

With an award winning career spanning 14 years, Bruce continues to be passionate about photography. When not shooting commercial work from his home town of Napier, he can be found anywhere around the country updating images for his own stock photo agency.

GRAEME JENNINGS

Describes his work as classically unorthodox. He is a recent entry to the photographic field, but already his work has appeared in GEO, North and South and New Zealand The Millennium.

KAREN JOHNSON

See Southland Photographic Society.

ALAN KING

See Southland Photographic Society.

NEIL LIVERSEDGE

A creative photographer of 20 years experience, operating out of a 1910 community church in Auckland, Neil looks for the slightly surreal and for unique people happenings 'frozen in small moments of time'. Apart from restoring two old Citroens and a 1924 kauri mullet boat, he works on a mixture of corporate advertising and design assignments.

JOHN McCOMBE

Began his career as a cadet with The Thames Star and worked for five different newspapers. He was chief photographer on The Waikato Times and The Christchurch Star, and illustrations editor on the latter from 1987 to 1990, when he set up his own company. A most experienced and competent photo-journalist, he has a great love for the west coast of the South Island.

ANTHONY McKEE

Is a Christchurch based editorial photographer, specialising in documentary and portrait images. He is the author of two major exhibitions, The Oamaru Mail, a review of life in small town NZ, and In Our Own Land, a study of the Chatham Islands.

GEOFF MASON

A major contributor to our original DITLONZ, Geoff is probably one of the best known and best credentialled of NZ photographers, with many books and magazine contributions to his credit. He is widely published all over the world.

HAROLD MASON

Has been a professional photographer for over 30 years. Trained as a photojournalist, he opened his own studio in Christchurch and 15 years ago moved to Nelson. Recent assignments have taken him throughout New Zealand and Europe. He is a former president of the NZIPP.

MIKE MATTHEW

Mike's inventive approach to photography, combined with years of digital imaging, design and dark room magic, produces a distinctive graphic style. His optimistic approach and passion for balance and motion are evident in his photographs of yoga, dance and white-water kayaking.

ANNE MEIN

Says she found Auckland not sufficiently inspiring so moved to Milton in Otago! Having found her feet, she progressed to Dunedin. A diploma in fine arts whetted her appetite for exotic places so she spent three murky years on the tubes of London. Anne now works as a freelancer back in Auckland.

LEIGH MITCHELL-ANYON

Since 1961, Leigh has operated Texta Studios in Wanganui. During this time, he has gained a Bachelor of Fine Arts and a Master of Photography (NZIPP) and in the 90's won numbers of photographic awards.

AVIS MOUNTAIN

Has lived most of her life in the Bay of Islands. For the past 32 years, with husband Bill, she has farmed on the beautiful Purerua Peninsula, surrounded by the sea which inspired many of her early photos. Twelve years ago, she expanded her photographic hobby and joined a local camera club. She has been an active member ever since, holding various positions, including president for five years, and has been successful in outside competitions.

GEOFF O'BRIEN

Has been for the last 20 years a freelance documentary photographer based in Christchurch. He has photographed and travelled widely in Asia, the Middle East and the Pacific. His work is published in a wide range of books and magazines and group photographic exhibitions held in NZ, Thailand, Japan and Iran.

DENIS PAGÉ

Canadian born, Denis has shot pretty much everything under the sun, from sharks to Elle McPherson. Having moved to New Zealand eight years ago to seek fame and fortune, he specialises in editorial, travel and natural history photography around the world. His work has been published in books and CD-Rom and his by-line noted by major world companies.

RHYS PALMER

A self-employed commercial photographer, Rhys is Hamilton based, having formerly photographed for The Waikato Times and The New Zealand Herald.

LLOYD PARK

Was one of the participants in our original DITLONZ in 1983. A major prize winner in many national and international competitions, he has developed his distinctive style over 40 years of varied experience. His passion for photography has never diminished and from his base in an old church in Christchurch he is always in demand, with a client list of Who's Who in the New Zealand corporate and publishing worlds.

CHRIS PARKER

From the age of nine processing his own black and white prints, Chris has progressed to running studios in both Hamilton and Tauranga. Strongly involved with the NZIPP, his work takes him all over the country and overseas.

DAWN PATTERSON

See Southland Photographic Society.

CRAIG PERKINS

Self-employed in Timaru, Craig says: "Had my first camera at four years and took amazing images of foreheads and lots of sky. Now I get less sky. Love people photography and am a real medium format nut."

VLADIMIR PETROVIC

Was born in Belgrade and worked as a fashion and advertising photographer in Europe before emigrating to NZ in 1995. He is currently employed by the Woolf studio in Wellington and already his work has received a number of awards.

RON REDFERN

KEVIN WEIR

NICK SERVIAN

BOB TULLOCH

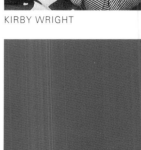

KIRBY WRIGHT

KIM REED

CYNTHIA VAN DE LOO

TREVOR WINKWORTH

TIM STEELE

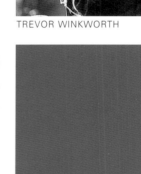

GILBERT VAN REENEN

STEPHEN ROBINSON

SIMON WOOLF

CHRIS ROLLINS

DAVID WALL

198

RICHARD POOLE

Is the NZ guru of black and white photography. He now spends the majority of his time teaching photography at Canterbury University. He has over 30 years experience in the craft, commencing in Timaru then Palmerston North, England and Australia before settling in Christchurch 20 years ago. He most enjoys people photography and is the leading scribe for *The Photographer's Mail* on matters black and white.

RON REDFERN

Started his career in photography in 1947. In the mid-50s he was in charge of the photographic section at the Dominion Physical Laboratory prior to managing a leading commercial studio in Wellington. He started his own studio in 1962 and has worked throughout NZ and the South Pacific Basin ever since. He looks forward to "... looking at life through a lens for another 50 years". Ron was a participant in our original *DITLONZ*.

KIM REED

Was born and raised in Las Vegas, Nevada. She studied photojournalism in Chicago and participated in the Eddie Adams Workshop in New York. Married to a Kiwi, Kim lives in Auckland and works as a freelance photographer and writer.

STEPHEN ROBINSON

Has been a freelancer for 12 years and still loves it, especially shooting people and food. Black and white holds a special fascination for him.

CHRIS ROLLINS

Has returned to NZ after a two year stint in the UK and is now studying photography full time. At 38, he says he's the oldest student and wants to portray the gay community in its positive aspects. Ambition: to photograph for *Vanity Fair*.

GRAEME SEDAL

Began his photography interest over 40 years ago. He tutors photography and works professionally in Auckland. His work features in numerous publications and he was also one of our original *DITLONZ* participants.

NICK SERVIAN

Began his career as a professional tourism photographer, for 12 years photographing the people and pageantry, the landscapes and architecture of Britain and Europe, especially the cathedrals and stately homes of England. Now has his own commercial studio in Wellington where corporate, advertising and travel photography are his passions. Nick was a participant in our original *DITLONZ*.

SOUTHLAND PHOTOGRAPHIC SOCIETY

Four keen amateurs have enthusiastically embraced the concept, as the results show. All dyed-in-the-wool Southlanders, some already have work published. They all worked tirelessly on the day.

TIM STEELE

Is the head of Fuji Professional in New Zealand. A 20-year photographic industry veteran, he has also worked as a commercial photographer specialising in the editorial and illustrative fields. His photographs have been published in *Focus on New Zealand, Salute to New Zealand*, promotional brochures for the Fiji Islands and in a number of leading magazines.

KEVIN STENT

Based in Wellington, Kevin is currently a staff photographer for *The Sunday Star Times*. He has been a press photographer for over 10 years.

GERAR TOYE

Describes himself as a 'global gypsy' and 'imagist' with a spontaneous artistic style, travelling the planet for over 17 years.

BOB TULLOCH

Based in Tauranga, Bob operates a commercial studio with an emphasis on people photography. He has published a book on the Bay of Plenty, several calendars and is currently working on a series of portraits paying tribute to success stories in the local community. He is a past president and life member of the NZIPP.

CYNTHIA VAN DE LOO

Is a Rangiora-based freelancer. She studied photography at Canterbury University and while filming and producing with Diage Multimedia, a TV production company, held artistic photographic exhibitions. She is the winner of numerous awards and is already a well-respected industry figure.

GILBERT VAN REENEN

Was born in Indonesia and schooled in Invercargill. Gilbert developed his photographic interest on numerous expeditions into Fiordland. He completed his veterinary degree at Massey University and has practised throughout the South Island, including three years as a full time deer specialist during the heyday of the helicopter deer-capture industry. He has been based in Wanaka since 1981 where he combines the occupation of professional photographer with that of a vet-scientist and is currently a member of the Otago Conservation Board.

DAVID WALL

Runs his own extensive photo library in Dunedin, supplying images of New Zealand and Africa to national and international publications. David has several successful major books to his credit.

TREFOR WARD

Is originally from Cardiff, Wales, where he gained his diploma from the Swansea College of Art. His work has appeared in major magazines throughout Europe and NZ and he has held 15 exhibitions in the UK and NZ, as well as photographing for several notable books.

KEVIN WEIR

One of the enthusiastic, talented amateurs participating in our project, Kevin is a Mosgiel based landscape designer and contractor. A lover of the outdoors, he regularly hunts and fishes, always accompanied by his camera.

TONY WHINCUP

Has worked extensively as a photographer in Britain, Uganda and Kiribati and is currently head of photography at Massey University in NZ. His work is in both private and public collections and in numerous publications. He is at present working on a book documenting the traditional dancing of Kiribati.

TREVOR WINKWORTH

One of life's enthusiasts, Trevor has organised several major photographic exhibitions displayed in New Zealand consulates world-wide. A successful participant in our original *DITLONZ*, his work has appeared in every field of photography.

SIMON WOOLF

Is a Wellington based photographer who has been involved in what was a family business almost since birth. Simon has undertaken assignments in NZ and overseas, has gained numerous awards locally and internationally, and has a special attraction to photographing people, landscapes and nature. He holds qualifications in NZ, Australia and the USA, exhibits frequently and also judges and writes on photography regularly. Photography is both his profession and recreation.

KIRBY WRIGHT

Another of the very successful contributors to our original *DITLONZ*, Kirby commenced photography in 1953 in New Plymouth. Since then, he has worked on both sides of the Tasman in the fields of fashion, commercial, technical, and editorial. For the past eight years he has freelanced from Hamilton.

ANTARCTIC DIVISION

Antarctica New Zealand Pictorial Collection Photographer Dean Arthur

Also:
LYNN CLAYTON
MEGAN HALL
NOEL HALL
BOB HUNTER
KURT LANGER
CECILE TAIT

Notes from Malcolm McGregor

Working on a book of this nature is a matter of intense pride and a feeling of love of country. To look through and edit 25,000 shots from all over the nation cannot fail to impress with the diversity of people and countryside and make you feel how fortunate we are compared with the rest of the world.

Although 12 months in the planning, this has been a daunting project logistically, travelling the length of New Zealand several times, viewing portfolios, arranging locations, subjects and permissions. Yet after all this the weather on the day was the problem we couldn't control. Auckland fireworks proved a disappointment, The Gathering at Takaka was rained out, the Auckland Cup was postponed for the first time in its history and rain in areas over much of the country spoiled various planned shoots. But if that was the state of the nation on the day, then that was the way we had to present it. Nevertheless, most photographers triumphed over adversity and our difficulty has been more what to leave out than what to include.

Without intending to, such an exercise becomes a little competitive between participants. Not only that, but it is extremely taxing, many photographers going without sleep for 36 hours or more in order to cover the complete 24 hour period. There is also an element of excitement and challenge about the day, no better illustrated than comments from participants…

"I really meant to restrict myself to six or seven subjects, but I just couldn't help myself. Having countered the stress, I went into 'go' mode. It was such an amazing opportunity I just wanted to make the most of it."

"Almost all my time was spent in rain. Fortunately I found a plastic bag which I was able to tape around my camera and protect it from water damage. It was very difficult to set the exposures correctly. Every time I needed to change a film I had to cut the bag open. And I had only slept two hours the night before, I was so excited about the project!"

"It was a very intense 24 hours. I loved it and hated it all at once but I am so glad I was involved."

"Unfortunately the weather was a pig. But I had a ball and so did the people I photographed along the way. Thanks heaps!"

"Couldn't complete all my record sheets because a guy alongside me collapsed and I had to accompany him to the hospital."

"Had a wonderful day. Enjoyed meeting such a diverse group of people - a great way to start off the first day of the millennium."

"This has been one hell of an experience! If you ever have another such project, please give me a call."

This reflects the spirit of a wonderful group of talented people whose co-operation and friendship made the exercise so enjoyable. Having published the original 'A Day in the Life of New Zealand' in 1983, I felt we had covered the topic. Yet the record for posterity of our nation in action on this most celebrated New Year in our lifetimes was too strong to resist. A once in a thousand years' opportunity!

Our hope is that future generations will value this book in their understanding of life in New Zealand at the beginning of the 21st century. A footprint in history!

We would all like to thank the public in general for their ready assistance, so generously given, but specifically we must acknowledge Jane Connor and the staff at Random House, Tony Moffatt, Air New Zealand, Hanimex, Auckland Coast Guard, Margaret and Ian Moffatt, Terri and Lloyd Park and Denis Callesen. Overall, the production of this volume has been smoothed by the advice, skill and dedication of Mark and Irene Garner, as well as Joe Kosac. The enthusiasm and ready co-operation of Brian Curtis, our co-ordinator, carried the team forward at all times and I cannot express strongly enough my gratitude to him and his wife Deb.

AUCKLAND

DUNEDIN

CHRISTCHURCH

WELLINGTON